C000061020

Published by:

Just Perfect Analysing Ltd.
PO Box 1129
Bedford MK40 4XT

Examples of writing have been used in this book to illustrate
a particular point and do not represent a full analysis.
The interpretations supplied under each section do not
necessarily apply to the writer and no personal criticism of the
character is intended. The text supplied with each handwriting
sample reflects the professional opinion of the author.

Designed and illustrated by Tony Ososki, Winslow, Buckingham
Printed by Print Concern Limited, Cowley, Oxford

ISBN 978-0-9555045-0-1

The Ultimate Guide to
Handwriting Analysis

Joyce Parkinson **MBIG (Dip)**

Family, friends,
workmates, strangers...
...their personalities
revealed by their
handwriting!

Published by **Just Perfect Analysing Limited**

CONTENTS Page No

CONTENTS

Chapter 1   **Introduction**

Introduction

If you have an interest in people and what makes them 'tick', you'll be captivated by the contents of this book. It's not just about graphology and what the handwriting movements mean; read on and discover a new insight into human behaviour and personality traits. Readers will begin to view themselves, their family, friends and work colleagues in a new light.

The reason I decided to write this book is because of the variety of characters I have encountered over the years. I wanted to show how personalities are reflected in handwriting movements and to introduce complete novices to the subject (see Chapter 2). The intention is to promote interest in the analysis of handwriting (graphology) and its uses so that newcomers are inspired to learn more. I have discovered that people generally know very little about the subject, so hopefully the contents of this book will widen knowledge and understanding. There is also a message of personal development.

People are always fascinated to learn how I became involved with such an unusual subject. It began many years ago. My working life started off as an office junior and I gradually worked my way up to a Personal Assistant.

My secretarial career provided the golden opportunity to work with a variety of people at all levels and I became fascinated by all the different personality types I encountered. Some of the handwriting proved challenging to read but I never realised that it was possible to produce a character analysis from the scrawl I encountered.

My interest in graphology was triggered by chance when I read an article on the subject. Some years later I noticed a graphology correspondence course advertised in the national press and I immediately jumped at the chance to study this unusual subject. I became hooked as I gradually worked my way through the course and began to see people and handwriting in a new light.

Having started the course purely as a casual interest, I soon realised that I could be on the road to a new vocation. My transition began when I had the opportunity to take voluntary redundancy from my last full-time role as a Personal Assistant. The money gave me the spring-board to spend more time on my studies and get qualified. At intervals I took temporary assignments which brought me into contact with even more interesting people and their handwriting. As soon as I saw the writing of the person or people I was working with, it gave me an immediate insight into their behaviour and how they worked. I have picked up so much knowledge this way which has added to my expertise.

I realised my dream when I completed the course and passed 6 difficult exams to obtain my diploma. I'd always wanted to work for myself, so I feel very fortunate to own my company, Just Perfect Analysing Ltd. I have an interesting and unique career too!

History/Research

The analysis of handwriting dates back many centuries to Roman times with evidence coming from Chinese and Greek sources. In 1622 the first book on the subject 'How to recognise from a letter the nature and quality of a writer' was written by Italian philosopher, Camillo Baldo.

Research officially began in France during the early 19th Century when a group of monks under Abbé Michon gathered together thousands of samples and started to put interpretations on the movements. At first they started to put fixed interpretations on each movement, e.g. large writing indicates an extrovert or small writing an introvert. In 1871, after 40 years of painstaking research, the term 'Graphology' was established in France and it was put on a scientific footing.

Research continued and one of Michon's students, Jule Crepieux-Jamin, realised that one movement and interpretation on its own were not fixed. He discovered that at least three movements were required with the same meaning to confirm a trait, e.g. large size, right slant and broad letters indicate confidence. The purpose of this book is to take the reader from simply understanding individual movements and interpretations (Chapter 2) to more adventurous linking and personality types (Chapters 4 & 5).

Further research has taken place in other Western European countries where the Germans became world leaders. Consequently, it is quite common in France and Germany for candidates to have their handwriting analysed when applying for a job. Over the years Graphology has been validated by researchers in other countries such as the USA and Japan.

How does graphology work?

Graphologists call the act of writing 'brainwriting' because of the message which is passed from the brain to the hand to form movements on the page. An interesting comparison is to describe it as static body language which has been literally frozen on the page. What is revealed is a 'snap-shot' of the writer's personality, moods and emotions at the time of writing.

Everyone's writing style is unique to them, just like a fingerprint. The process begins at school when we learn to write and at first we consciously concentrate on forming letters in a set style. Once these basic outlines are mastered, then the process of writing becomes automatic and unconscious. It is then that personality traits emerge in our own unique style of writing.

A graphologist follows precise rules in order to construct a detailed analysis. Movements are scrutinised and measured; interpretations assigned and a personality profile gradually emerges. It's a bit like constructing a huge jigsaw puzzle. Our extensive training provides us with the expertise to decide what is applicable and what is not. The result is an accurate analysis which provides a remarkable insight into the writer.

Code of Ethics

The training I have undertaken with the British Institute of Graphologists ensures that information is relayed as sensitively as possible. In this way writers are more inclined to accept and make changes in their lives where certain issues need to be addressed. The Institute asks members to sign a Code of Ethics to ensure a high standard of ethical behaviour and performance is adhered to.

Chapter 2 **Lesson**

Now on to the interesting part of
learning about the movements
and gaining a basic understanding of
their meaning.   There are literally
hundreds of movements if you take
each individual formation into
account such as 'i' dots and 't' bars.
These are what we call miscellaneous
movements and they only provide us with a
small amount of the information.   Primarily, we are more concerned
with what is happening all the time in the writing such as size, slant,
pressure, letter shapes, connectedness, rhythm and layout. These are
regarded as dominant factors and have the most influence on any
analysis. The knowledge gained in this section will provide the reader
with a good understanding of the main movements before looking at
personality types covered in Chapters 4 and 5.

The aim of this lesson is to encourage beginners to start to recognise
movements for themselves without getting too involved with the
measuring process. Professional graphologists are trained to follow a
set procedure which begins with scrutinizing the movements, often
using a magnifying glass.   The next stage is to ensure that exact
measurements are taken so that correct interpretations are made.
This involves drawing lines on the handwriting to aid measurement of
the various movements and letter shapes. First take a photocopy and
then draw the lines on the copy or place the original under tracing
paper. Avoid marking the original otherwise it will soon become
unrecognisable due to the number of lines drawn all over it.

PLEASE NOTE: It is important to point out that each movement has a list of interpretations. In many instances you will see that there are two columns giving positive and negative traits. Not all the interpretations apply to a particular individual, so it is down to the expertise of the graphologist to decide which ones apply. Therefore, my advice is to apply those given under 'Positive and General Meanings' and only use the negative ones sparingly because they only apply in certain circumstances. It is also important to emphasise that the handwriting samples provided in each section are meant to illustrate a particular aspect such as size, slant etc. and are there solely for that purpose. A full analysis is required to give a complete picture of the individual which puts traits into their correct context.

Chapter 2(a) **Size & Zones**

SIZE

If the writing is noticeably large or small, the follow procedure can be omitted.   The explanation has been included so that readers can appreciate the care taken to ensure exact measurements are taken.

Measuring the overall size: Look for letters with upper and lower zone extensions which appear anywhere in the word.   Find the letter which extends furthest into the upper zone and draw a line which extends across the top of the word.   Then look for a letter which extends into the lower zone and draw a line across the bottom of the whole word.   Lastly, measure the distance between the lines. **Please note that words beginning with capitals cannot be used.**

Large size over 11.5mm   Outgoing and confident

Small size under 8.5mm   Reserved and modest

Medium size 8.5mm-11.5mm   Balanced approach, conventional attitudes

The overall size of the writing indicates the degree of confidence a person has. This includes how the individual relates to others and the outside world. For instance, if you know someone with a larger-than-life character, then their writing is likely to be large. This is because the larger the writing the more extrovert, outgoing and confident the person is going to be and their traits are quite obvious to spot.

Smaller writing indicates reserve and modesty but it is often the case that such writers are contracting their personality so that their traits are well hidden. There is much more to this writer than immediately comes to light and can be compared to a tin of condensed soup or an iceberg. So, don't underestimate someone with small writing!

Medium sized writing often points towards a balance between the two with more emphasis on traditional values and a conservative outlook.

Large Overall Size - Over 11.5mm

Large Size

POSITIVE OR GENERAL MEANINGS

Adventurous	Leadership ability
Ambitious	Loves action
Enjoys life to the full	Needs freedom and hates restrictions
Enthusiastic	
Expansive	Outgoing
Extrovert	Sees the big picture
Generous	Strong sense of self
	Wide range of interests and friends

NEGATIVE

Boastful about accomplishments

Conceited with strong sense of self-importance (very large size)

Extravagant

Prone to distraction

Lack of self-discipline

Poor attention to detail

Small Overall Size - under 8.5mm

Have you ever met someone who has left you
with an unusual feeling, a sense of 'won
and not just because of their physical bea
but because of that 'thing' - something
intangible that makes that person speci
to you? I have. I saw it, felt it, and
realised it, even before I knew her!

Small Size

POSITIVE OR GENERAL MEANINGS

Ability to concentrate on detail
Ability to enjoy own company
Accurate and careful
Conscientious
Introverted - contracts personality
Modest and unassuming

NEGATIVE

Frugal
Lack of confidence
Self-limiting outlook on life

Medium Overall Size - 8.5-11.5mm

It reminds me that, just as springtime
follows winter, light will follow dark an
good times. will follow bad . And so th
cycle repeats. It's the wheel of life It's
inevitable ! Behind the clouds the s

Medium Size

POSITIVE OR GENERAL MEANINGS

Conventional
Good judgment
Well balanced

ZONES

upper zone u/z

middle zone m/z

lower zone l/z

handwriting

Once the overall size of the writing is determined, the next important step is to look at the individual zones. Each zone is associated with the personality traits given below in this section. Ideally each zone should be roughly equal in measurement, e.g. 3mm. Where this happens the zones are regarded as balanced and so is the personality. However, it is quite rare to see such balanced zones. It is usually the case that one zone is bigger than the rest which indicates an emphasis in that particular area of the personality.

Equally, when a particular zone is smaller, this indicates that less importance is placed in that area or there may be a degree of inadequacy. For instance, someone who has a smaller lower zone with a larger upper zone will be more concerned with intellectual and spiritual matters over materialistic longings.   The writer of a small middle zone can have poor self-esteem and will compensate by extending the upper and lower zones. This increases the overall size of the writing and in turn their confidence levels.

Upper Zone Emphasis (u/z)

What a selection of weather we experienced today. We left in clear bright sun but soon hit fog on the hill. This stayed with us until we

POSITIVE OR GENERAL MEANINGS	NEGATIVE
Idealistic	Fantasy
Intellectual	Too idealistic
Intuitive	
Spiritual	

Middle Zone Emphasis (m/z)

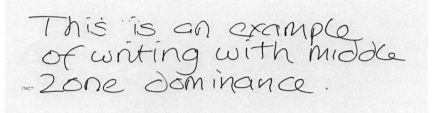

POSITIVE OR GENERAL MEANINGS

Extroversion
Leadership potential
Self-assured
Strong personality

NEGATIVE

Concerned with self
Domineering
Inability to concentrate for
long periods of time

Lower Zone Emphasis (l/z)

POSITIVE OR GENERAL MEANINGS
Active and energetic
Drive and determination
Physical and materialistic desires
Practical
Sensuous

NEGATIVE

Overly materialistic
Restlessness

Chapter 2(b) **Slant**

The slant is the second major movement we look at because it indicates social and emotional expression.

The measuring process

In the early stages of studying, a trainee graphologist will use a protractor to measure the exact degree of slant. To do this, choose a few letters with long upper and lower zone extensions and draw a line with a ruler down that letter (as illustrated). Then place the protractor over the letter to measure the slant. As experience grows, the slant is immediately apparent. However, if there is a lot of variation, it is wise to measure a selection of letters to ascertain the dominant slant.

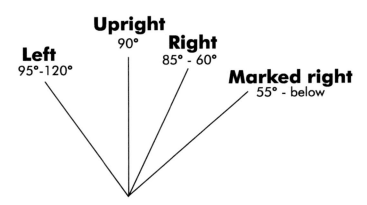

Upright
90°

Left
95°-120°

Right
85° - 60°

Marked right
55° - below

Right Slant (85°- 60°)

The right slanted writer is more inclined to seek out the company of other people. It is almost as if they are leaning forwards towards others and the outside world. The further over to the right the slant tilts, the more emotionally expressive the writer will be. This is especially true of the marked right slant writer and it is quite usual for this type to instantly react with tears, laughter or even a hot temper! However, a slight right slant (as shown below) indicates that the writer is more in control of their emotions and not so explosive!

I have just told the exhibition
lady that I heard her on
3 counties Radio . I also
said that I work and it
is a bit hit and miss
if I catch the Radio

Right Slant (85°- 60°)

POSITIVE OR GENERAL MEANINGS	NEGATIVE
Adaptable	Can be hasty and lack control
Communicative	Easily distracted
Demonstrative but not overly emotional	
Extrovert	
Optimism	
Sociable and warm disposition	

Marked Right Slant (55° - below)

> *I am very much looking forwa*
> *to meeting up with you both*
> *again this summer for a*

Marked Right Slant (55° - below)

POSITIVE OR GENERAL MEANINGS | NEGATIVE

Passionate and likely to feel
strongly about certain issues
Very demonstrative

Easily hurt
Lack of discipline
Liable to act before thinking
Overly emotional and easily
shows feelings
Restlessness

Upright Slant (90° but can vary between 85°- 95°)

The writer of an upright style is likely to be more independent with
emotions kept under control.   They can appear cool, calm and
collected and are often very good in an emergency because they don't
panic.

> *There are few things in this life as beautiful*
> *as flowers. And springtime is such a*
> *spectacular canvas for them! Magnolia*
> *trees, cherry blossom, waving daffodils,*
> *fragrant hyacinths, trees bursting with*
> *fresh green buds. Wonderful.*

Upright (90° but can vary between 85° - 95°)

<u>POSITIVE OR GENERAL MEANINGS</u>

Cautious
Cool and calm in an emergency
Head before the heart
Independent and self-assured
Logical
Objective and impartial judgment
Reserved
Sees both sides of an argument

<u>NEGATIVE</u>

Can appear aloof and unfeeling
Frugal
Indifferent
Pessimistic and prone to disillusionment
Uncommunicative

Left Slant (95°- 120°)

In theory, the left slant indicates someone who is more reserved but often other movements counteract this influence. For instance, you might have a friend who appears very outgoing but underneath there is some self-doubt or they may actually like to have time alone to recharge their batteries. Sometimes it can indicate a desire to be different. As far as emotions are concerned, they don't readily show them. In short, the left slant can be difficult to explain, although I have listed a few commonly known traits below.

Left Slant (95°-120°)

POSITIVE OR GENERAL MEANINGS

NEGATIVE

Can work alone

Cautious about showing feelings

Keeps things private

Persistent

Polished public image

Inwardly focussed

Lack of spontaneity

Overly controlled and cautious

Self-conscious

Mixed Slant (varying left/upright/right)

A mixed slant represents an individual who can be rather moody and changeable as they fluctuate between introversion (left slant), extroversion (right slant) and independence (upright)

Mixed Slant (varying left/upright/right)

POSITIVE OR GENERAL MEANINGS

NEGATIVE

Highly adaptable

Changeable and moody
Unpredictable

Chapter 2(c) **Pressure & Thickness of Pen**

PRESSURE

The pressure is the third most important thing that a graphologist looks at because it denotes the writer's physical strength, energy and vitality.

The way that we gauge it is to turn the writing over and rub our fingers over the back of the sheet.   If there are definite writing indentations formed by the writing, the pressure is medium or high and so will the writer's energy.   If you know of someone who is always busy and active or can party all night and still get up fresh in the morning ready to face another busy day, then they are likely to have heavy pressure. However, if there are no indentations, the pressure is light which can be found in rather reserved but often highly intelligent, sensitive and cultured individuals.   It also points towards lighter energy levels, so this type is likely to feel tired by the end of the day and probably feels happier working in short bursts.

PLEASE NOTE: Pressure should not be confused with stroke thickness which is covered next.

Light pressure = reduced energy levels

Light Pressure

POSITIVE OR GENERAL MEANINGS

Cultural interests
Flexible, easily adapts
Idealistic outlook
Less physically intense (not violent)
Modesty
Sensitive nature
Spiritual

NEGATIVE

Lack of stamina
Poor resistance to pressure
Weak energy levels
Weak libido

Medium pressure = average energy

Medium Pressure

POSITIVE OR GENERAL MEANINGS

Emotional control
Endurance and stamina
Flexible, easily adapts
Good energy and vitality levels
Warm disposition

Heavy pressure = high energy

Heavy Pressure

POSITIVE OR GENERAL MEANINGS   NEGATIVE

Ability to control emotions and impulses   Aggressive
Active with high energy levels   Obstinate
Determined to succeed
Initiative
Strong endurance
Vital and durable

Very heavy pressure = intense

Very Heavy Pressure

POSITIVE OR GENERAL MEANINGS   NEGATIVE

Very strong willpower and   Domineering - uses undue force
determination   Frustrated
Very persistent   Intense
        Temperamental
        Violent and brutal nature
        Will not allow obstacles in path

STROKES - THICKNESS OF PEN

The thickness of the pen indicates the natural degree of inner warmth or coolness in an individual. As mentioned above, pressure and pen thickness should not be confused. This is because it is possible to have a thick looking (pasty stroke) with light pressure and a thin looking (sharp stroke) with heavy pressure.

Pasty Stroke

This stroke is thicker and associated with a warm and sensuous nature. These writers tend to experience everything through the senses - touch, taste, smell, hearing and sight, so good food, drink and sex are important factors in their lives. They have a great capacity for enjoyment and appreciate a good standard of living. A camping holiday in the middle of a muddy field would probably not suit this type.

Pasty

POSITIVE OR GENERAL MEANINGS	NEGATIVE
Ability to absorb shock	Excessive self-indulgence
Capacity for enjoyment	Lack of spiritual values
Deep and ardent emotions	Lazy disposition
Easygoing, warm personality	Materialistic
Free and easy disposition	Prone to self-indulgence
Realistic outlook	Undisciplined
Visually orientated	Uninhibited
Warm and sensuous	

Sharp Stroke

This stroke is clean and sharply executed and is associated with spiritual awareness. The sharp writer has the ability to see things very clearly and to express themselves articulately. They can be considered cold because their approach is often reserved with an emphasis on refinement. They prefer jobs to be done properly and make judgments in terms of black or white with no middle ground. This type may not seem to enjoy life quite as much as the pasty writer.

> *This is a sample of my normal (not calligraph
handwriting. If I try really hard I can produce quite
acceptable calligraphy, but this is easier and faster
If I'm just making notes for myself, my writing
is much more of a scrawl, and sometimes almost*

Sharp

POSITIVE OR GENERAL MEANINGS	NEGATIVE
Aesthetic appreciation	Critical
Articulate	Emotionally cold
Clear thought processes	Lack of realism
Discriminate	Low threshold for shock
High standards	Prone to anxiety
Idealistic	
Refined nature	
Reserved	
Self-disciplined	
Sensitive	
Spiritual	
Strong sense of right and wrong	

Distinct Stroke

This stroke is formed with a thick down and thin upstroke which indicates someone who is concerned with how things look, so they have aesthetic appreciation and artistic flair.   Their outlook is more traditional but they can be relied upon to have emotional balance.

> A few weeks ago I went to the wedding of a girl I have worked with. A girl I have liked and admired + made a friend of. In fact, since my first days of working for the Company I have known her + took to her niceness + warmth.

Distinct

POSITIVE OR GENERAL MEANINGS

Aesthetic appreciation/artistic flair
Articulate
Flexible
Reliable
Traditional outlook
Well integrated & distinctive personality with emotional balance

Chapter 2(d)   Connectedness & Letter Width

CONNECTEDNESS

connected

The way the letters *disconnected*
are linked together
in a word relates to thought processes and
mental abilities.   For instance, connected
letters indicate continuous thought patterns,
whereas disconnection involves a break in the
natural flow.   However, it is not always the case
that writing is totally connected or disconnected
and it can be difficult to determine which category the writing falls into.
We begin by looking at a reasonably long word and the rule to follow
is that if no more than 3 letters are disconnected, then the writing is
mainly connected.   If no more than 3 letters in that long word are
connected, then the writing is mainly disconnected.

Connected Letters

Someone with mainly connected writing will prefer to work on a task
from beginning to end without interruption.   If they have too many
breaks in concentration they are likely to lose their train of thought.   If
you try and talk to this type whilst their mind is otherwise occupied,
then you are wasting your time because they won't hear you.   I once
worked for a manager who had very connected writing and he even
linked some of his words as well.   He would get really engrossed with
his thoughts and rarely noticed if you walked into his office, so it was
often difficult to get his attention.   His workload often meant dealing
with very complicated matters, so he was well placed in being able to
concentrate for long periods of time.

Today I am not very busy. The main hassle has been to cancel a social arrangement in Brighton for the weekend of 17/18 September. Instead I made an arrangement to travel home from 30th Sept to 03 Oct.

Connected

POSITIVE OR GENERAL MEANINGS

Ability to concentrate
Ability to plan and organise
Consistent behaviour
Continuous thought processes
Flexible
Purposeful attitude
Systematic and logical

NEGATIVE

Can get too caught up with own ideas (one track mind)
Hates interruptions
Poor observation

Disconnected Letters

Disconnected writers cope well with interruptions because they can easily go back and pick up the threads of a task they left earlier on. However, they can easily get distracted because they are receptive and open to what is happening around them. People of this type are often intuitive because they pick up on all sorts of things happening around them which the connected writer would miss.

The house is situated in a quiet terraced street. It dates back to the Victorian era & is currently in need of modernization. The kitchen is particularly bad and will need to be

Disconnected

POSITIVE OR GENERAL MEANINGS	NEGATIVE
Can cope with interruptions	Easily distracted
Independent	Has trouble linking experiences
Individualistic style and behaviour	Introverted and withdrawn
Needs variety	Short attention span
Open to the thoughts & feelings of others	
Reliance upon instinct and intuition	

Mixture of Connected/Disconnected - no dominant

It is not uncommon for writing to be a mixture of both with no dominant apparent, so a mixture of interpretations can apply. However, I have found individuals with this mixture to be more adaptable as they seem to have the best of both worlds.

My life of crime, by arch criminal Manners, began at the age of † when I escaped from mother a ran off down Brackhill Drive i B only to be found by police and brought home i squad car ...

Connected/Disconnected

POSITIVE OR GENERAL MEANINGS

Creative
Flexible
Individualistic style and behaviour
Sensitive nature
Unconventional

NEGATIVE

Impatient and prone to
irritability

LETTER WIDTH

The width of the letters denotes the amount of expansion (extroversion) or restriction (introversion) within the personality and our attitude towards the outside world.   The first letters to be assessed are 'n' and 'u', followed by ovals.

Copymodel Width

We were taught to write with a copymodel width which means that the letters are as wide as they are high (e.g. 3mm x 3mm). A person who has maintained this width will have a more traditional outlook on life or some aspects of their personality will adhere to convention.

**Examples of copymodel
width 2.5mm x 2.5mm
3mm x 3mm**

" The quick brown fox jumps over
the lazy dog."

As you know, It contains every letter
of the alphabet - So very apt for
my work.

It was also set to music for our
choir as part of a musical.

Copymodel

POSITIVE OR GENERAL MEANINGS

Likes conventional situations

Broad Width

n o u

The wider the letters, the more expansive the personality is going to be. It's as if the writer is extending themselves towards other people and the outside world. This type has a generous and spontaneous disposition, so they easily mix with others. In a workplace situation they need to work where they are meeting other people even if they prefer to have their own area of responsibility.

> The weather is very
> kind to us with sun
> every day. We are
> having a wonderful
> time up. in scotland
> out walking every day.

Broad

POSITIVE OR GENERAL MEANINGS	NEGATIVE
Ability to accept advice	Careless
Adventurous	Impatient/impulsive
Ambitious	Inconsiderate
Courage and boldness	Lack of economy
Extrovert and sociable	Lack of self-control (extreme width)
Generous and friendly approach	Prone to exaggerate
Goal minded	Tactlessness
Open minded	
Prepared to try new ideas	
Progressive	
Spontaneity	

Narrow Width

n u

Narrow letters indicate restriction in some way and the writer is more cautious in their attitudes, particularly where relationships are concerned.   This type will often be secretly eyeing up new acquaintances and they will be reluctant to commit themselves immediately.

special in her life. She had a couple of
failed romances behind her which I think
had 'wised her up' in many ways + she
certainly had no illusions about the opposite
sex. More an attitude of not suffering fools
gladly. I really wondered if there was going
to be anyone out there for her, there surely
must be but there seemed lack of opportun

Narrow

POSITIVE OR GENERAL MEANINGS	NEGATIVE
Cautious	Anxiety
Considerate	Inhibition
Dependable	Overly cautious
Economical	Repression
Moderate behaviour	
Often shy	
Reserve and restraint	
Self-controlled	
Tactfulness	

Chapter 2(e)   **Letter Shapes & Styles**

FORMS OF CONNECTION
(letter shapes and styles)

Forms of connection refer to
the way a writer shapes their letters. For instance,
some styles look rounder and softer, whilst others
look pointed and harsh. These letter shapes reveal a
great deal about the writer's approach to life, general personality type,
attitudes and how they relate to other people. Begin by looking at the
way the letters 'n' and 'u' are shaped and then progress on to other
letters such as 'h', 'm' & 'w'. Sometimes it is difficult to ascertain the letter
shape because it is not clearly formed. You may also notice that some
people have a combination of letter formations which can be difficult to
interpret.

Arcades

An arcade is formed like an arch and in some cases even the letter 'u'
looks like an 'n'. The formation could be compared to placing a
protective roof over a structure, so anyone using this formation is
seeking to protect their emotions. Whilst the arcade writer is friendly
and can get on with most types, they are actually rather reserved. They
tend to keep their thoughts to themselves, so can be guarded and even
secretive. Where the arcade shape is precisely formed, this indicates
that the writer is also precise and exact in their actions. If you work for
an arcade writer, don't expect an easy life.   They work hard to
accomplish high standards and expect the same from others.

> " The quick brown fox jumps over
> the lazy dog "
> As you know, It contains every letter
> of the alphabet - so very apt for
> my work.
> It was also set to music for our
> choir as part of a musical

Arcades

POSITIVE OR GENERAL MEANINGS

Can keep a confidence
Cautious
Controlled emotions
Formal and traditional attitudes
Not easily influenced
Perfectionism
Reserved friendliness

NEGATIVE

Highly critical
Resistant to new ideas
Rigid, inflexible attitude
Secretive
Suspicious and distrustful

Garlands

u uu **Letters n & m**

This letter shape is soft and receptive; a bit like a cup and the letter 'n' looks like a 'u'. Garland writers are not competitive types and they hate confrontation. Their natural inclination is to avoid unpleasantness wherever possible, so they are usually easygoing and accommodating. They are often kind hearted and will go out of their way to help anyone in need, although they may feel taken advantage of at times.

It seems ages since I last wrote to you and there seems so much to catch up on. In the autumn I was made redundant which was

Garlands

POSITIVE OR GENERAL MEANINGS

Ability to compromise
Adaptable and accommodating
Emotionally expressive
Empathetic/understanding/tolerant
Generous, giving nature
Non-confrontational and yielding
Receptive and open
Warm, friendly and sociable

NEGATIVE

Dependency
Easily led, influenced and distracted
Lack of firm attitudes
Prone to immaturity
Weak-willed

Angles

Letters n u & m

This letter shape looks pointed and often appears quite harsh. In some cases the letter 'u' looks like a sharply executed 'n'. Angles represent firmness, aggression, decisiveness and determination, so it is usually associated with men's handwriting.   However, it can be adopted by women such as those who need firmness and courage to survive in their careers. The angular writer usually has good self-discipline and willpower which provides them with the ability to persevere with an unpleasant task until it is finished. If you come across this type, then you can expect excellent commitment but don't expect them to be tolerant because they don't suffer fools gladly.

Angles

POSITIVE OR GENERAL MEANINGS	NEGATIVE
Ability to plan and organise	Argumentative
Courageous	Cold and indifferent
Decisive and firm approach	Hardness
Direct and purposeful	Inflexible
Drive and determination	Lack of sympathy
Energetic	Overly forceful and aggressive
High moral standards	Resists other people's ideas and wishes
Persistent	Stubborn with rigid beliefs
Self-critical	
Self-control and willpower	
Sense of obligation and duty	

Thread

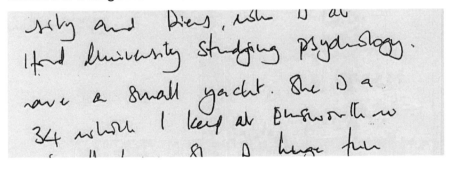

Letters n & m

Thread formations look like an uneven sinuous line which is formless. What is happening is that letter shapes are written at great speed and cut down to the bare minimum. Often this is caused by the mind rushing ahead and the hand struggling to keep up causing illegibility. This type is highly versatile and has the ability to 'go with the flow'. Also, threading is often seen in the handwriting of politicians as they 'duck and dive' to avoid awkward situations and present a diplomatic front. If you know of someone who hates being pinned down, it is likely that threads appear in their writing. This applies to individuals who have difficulty making firm decisions or commitments and are inclined to change their minds.

Thread

POSITIVE OR GENERAL MEANINGS

Diplomat or negotiator *(threading towards end of word)*
Genius *(with legibility)*
Highly adaptable
Intuitive
Many sided personality
Quick mind thinking ahead of actions

NEGATIVE

Lacks commitment
Undisciplined and
unpredictable

Primary Thread (Mixed Forms of Connection)

The main letter shapes have been covered, although writers often use a combination of arcades, angles, garlands and threads. If there are at least three, this mixture is usually referred to as Primary Thread. Often it is the case that threading is common in this type of script and so much of what has been said above applies. However, the exact interpretation depends on the mixture of shapes but these writers usually have an agile mind which easily switches direction and so do the letter formations.

The primary thread writer hates any form of restrictions and must be free to express their individuality and creativity. These formations are usually the sign of someone who is highly adaptable and ready for any situation.   Like the garland writer, they hate confrontations but the primary thread writer will use charm and a speedy mind to think of an easy solution. They are great opportunists because they don't hesitate or ponder for very long, so they are quick to take advantage of a situation.   In addition, they often have an instant understanding of others and can have an interest in psychology.

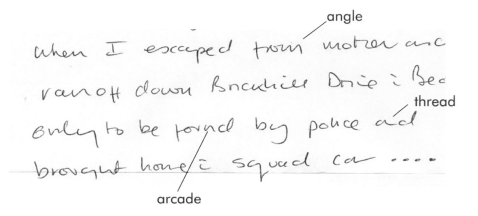

Primary Thread (mixed FOC)

POSITIVE OR GENERAL MEANINGS	NEGATIVE
Adaptable	Can take advantage of others
Creative ability	Lack of conscience and social
Interest in psychology and people	obligations
Opportunist	
Original thinking	
Quick mind	
Spontaneous	

STYLE - SIMPLIFICATION/ELABORATION

The style of the letters denotes our attitude towards life and how much detail we put into everyday life.

Simplification

Simplified letters are cut down to the essential with only the bare necessity of movement. If you know of someone who has a minimalist lifestyle this could apply to them. This movement is often linked with quick speed and high intelligence because the writer's thoughts are working at high speed whilst cutting out unnecessary detail and information. Therefore, they have the ability to quickly grasp essential information and to see where a shortcut would save time. These types can't wait to get started, so pleasantries can be overlooked and attention to detail is not their strong point.

Today is Friday – the end of the week. It's rain outside but surprisingly warm. Fancy it ser this kind of weather in September.

only to be found by police and brought home i squad car ..

In extreme cases where the letters are illegible, this is classed as 'neglect' (see sample below). This often happens when the writer is in a hurry, so the letter forms deteriorate. However, it can indicate deceit simply by being economical with the truth or a deliberate attempt to deceive. It requires the expertise of a graphologist to decide which is applicable.

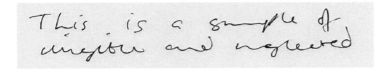

This is a sample of illegible and neglected

Simplified

POSITIVE OR GENERAL MEANINGS

Cuts actions down to the essential
Good judgment
Impartial
Purposeful
Quick grasp of the essential
Refined taste
Sense of order

NEGATIVE

Can be abrupt in haste to get things done
Lack of attention to detail
Lack of social form - tactless

NEGLECTED WRITING
(very illegible)
Deceptive
Slapdash

Elaboration

These writers are more concerned with life's pleasantries. If you know of someone who goes that extra mile to add detail to any aspect of their work, home life or appearance, they probably have some elaboration in their writing. Look out for flourishing pen movements which should be graceful and attractive.

Hear Joyce,
I have been wondering what
could write for you, and at last
Something Springs to mind!

Then one day along came a helping hand
a fairy godmother if you like, called Jackie

If the elaboration is taken to extremes with too many unnecessary movements, the interpretation is inclined to be negative (see sample below).

This is a sample of

POSITIVE OR GENERAL MEANINGS

Good social form and inter-personal skills

Pays attention to detail and all aspects of daily living

Sense of tradition

NEGATIVE

Desire to impress

Lack of good taste

Over-emphasis of formality

Prone to exaggeration

Chapter 2(f) **Layout**

The general layout reveals much about the writer's aesthetic tastes, their thought processes, how they relate to others and their attitude towards time. A graphologist will ask for handwriting samples to be supplied on plain paper so that margins, line space and direction can be assessed accurately. Each aspect of layout has its own interpretation which is covered in this chapter.

SPACING - WORDS

The spacing between the words indicates the writer's degree of sociability. For instance, someone with large spacing between each word wishes to place distance between themselves and other people. They may feel that others are invading their space and will soon back away. However, narrow word spacing represents the opposite and indicates that the writer needs contact with others. This type will often want to come up close and even touch another person. Where the word spacing is classed as normal, this indicates good interpersonal skills and the ability to get on with others.

Spacing between words:

Normal/Average: Good inter-personal and social skills.

An example of normal word spacing

Wide: Needs privacy and enjoys own company.

An example of wide spacing

Very Wide: Difficulty in establishing close relationships and fears intimate contact with others. Feels isolated.

Very wide word spacing

Narrow: Seeks constant social contact and closeness with others.

Narrow word spacing indicates a desire for company

Uneven Spacing: Alternately needs company and then needs privacy.

Uneven spacing with a mixture of

SPACING - LINES

The spacing between the lines reveals information about thought patterns and our sense of orderliness. In other words, how clearly we think and subsequently make plans.

Spacing between lines:

Narrow: A need for contact.   Confusion and a muddled mind (especially with line mingling).

> Close line spacing often results in mingling of The lower zone clothes

Normal or slightly wide: Clear mind, ability to plan and organise, inner balance and harmony.

> This is an example of normal and clear line spacing

Wide or Very wide: Out of touch, distrust, fear, isolation.

> when The line spacing is wide or very wide

BASELINE DIRECTION reflects our mood at the time of writing.

Rising: Ambition, buoyancy, enthusiasm, optimism.

Rising baselines optimistic

Horizonal: Composure, emotional stability, dependability, orderliness, self-control.

Horizontal lines

Falling: A sign of fatigue, depression, disappointment, discouragement.

Falling baselines

Undulating: Lack of self-control, mood changes, excitability.

undulating words and

Convex (arched): Inability to maintain stamina and enthusiasm.

convex or arched lines.

Concave (dipped in middle):   Fighter - able to overcome difficulties.

concave or dipping in middle

MARGINS represent the writer's attitude towards time, their pursuit of goals and social attitudes. Note: The right hand side of the page indicates the future, whilst the left relates to the past.

Equal/balanced margins all round: Aesthetic nature, artistic, aware of social boundaries, communicates clearly, consistent manner, sense of order and control.

Narrow left margin with wide right margin: Economical, informality, reflects on the past, often shy, reserved, wary of the future

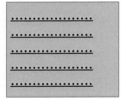

Wide left margin with narrow right margin: Ability to face life, cultural background, eager to communicate with others, generosity, moving away from the past, positive outlook towards the future, moving towards goals.

Narrow margins on both sides: Desire for popularity, informal attitudes, lack of taste, stinginess.

Wide margins on all 4 sides: Aesthetic outlook, may feel isolated, reserved.

Widening left margin: Enthusiasm, impatience, spontaneity.

Narrowing left margin: Cautious, drawn to the past, shy, suspicious nature.

Chapter 2(g)   Legibility/Regularity/Speed

It is easy for the complete beginner to confuse legibility, regularity and speed but they are three entirely separate areas. For instance, it would normally be assumed that carefully written letters would be very legible and this is normally true. However, this is not the case if the letters are very elaborate and I have often heard people complain about the illegibility of such writing. On the other hand, quick writers often have illegible writing because of the speed but it is possible to write quickly and still have legibility. Each section is covered separately in this chapter.

LEGIBILITY/ILLEGIBILITY

Writing is a form of communication, so if the letters are legible and it is easy to read, then the writer wishes to convey a clear message and to be understood. If the writing is illegible, it is often because the writer has a very quick mind and the pen can't keep up with their thoughts. This type of writer will often miss out letters and words. Often illegibility happens when we are making quick notes for ourselves which is natural. However, if the results are to be read by someone else, illegibility is a form of inconsiderateness towards the reader.

Legible Writing

> It reminds me that, just as springtime follows winter, light will follow dark and good times will follow bad. And so the

Legible

POSITIVE OR GENERAL MEANINGS

Clear communicators (speakers & teachers)
Clear judgment
Co-operative
Good taste
Mental clarity
Purposeful sense of order
Sincere and open

Illegible Writing

> This is a sample of unreadable and neglected

Illegible

POSITIVE OR GENERAL MEANINGS

Quick thinker

NEGATIVE

Carelessness, slapdash attitudes
Inconsiderate
Unco-operative
Unreliable

REGULARITY

Regular writing is neat and well ordered whilst irregular writing is erratic and probably looks rather untidy. The degree of regularity is affected by emotional feelings, so if the script is regular (or neat), good self-discipline is evident. The person is more likely to be stable and well ordered in their behaviour and punctual too. However, the opposite is true if the writing is very irregular (or untidy) because the writer does not have the same amount of self-control and hates too many restrictions. This type often has an attractive and likeable personality because of their free and easy manner.

Regular

Regular
POSITIVE OR GENERAL MEANINGS

Orderly and stable disposition
Predictable
Self-disciplined with good willpower
Sense of duty and reliability

NEGATIVE

(with too much rigidity)
Dogmatic
Inflexible and slow to adapt
Overly cautious and controlled

Slightly Irregular

Some slight irregularity in the script is an advantage because this type of person will have a flexible attitude to life and will be able to respond to changes without losing self-control.

> but because of that 'thing' – some thing intangible that makes that person spe to you? I have. I saw it, felt it an realised it, even before I knew her! I was fortunate as I also got to know her. to know her was to love her. To love a special soul, a beautiful soul.

Slightly Irregular

POSITIVE OR GENERAL MEANINGS

Lively personality
Mainly in control of emotions but maintains
flexible approach to life

Irregular

Irregular writing can have positive interpretations but the more pronounced the fluctuation, the more likely negative interpretations will apply. This is because irregular writers often feel off-centre with a general lack of self-control over their impulses.

My life of crime, by arch criminal Manners, began at the age of t when I escaped from mother a ran off down Breachill Drive i B only to be found by police and

Irregular

<u>POSITIVE OR GENERAL MEANINGS</u>

Can work from chaos

High degree of vivacity & spontaneity

Imaginative, creative mind

Propensity for new ideas

Very adaptable-loves variety/change

Warm nature

<u>NEGATIVE</u>

Disorderly and lacks self-control

Emotional and excitable

Hates too much routine

Impulsive and often headstrong

Irritable, moody, inconsistent

Poor concentration levels

Rather unpredictable

SPEED

We all have a natural in-built speed which governs how quickly our minds work and is carried through to our reactions and responses. For instance, some people take their time and prefer to act with caution, so the writing style is likely to be slower. The quick writer will often be in a hurry; they speak quickly and can act impulsively. The person with moderate thoughts and actions is likely to have medium paced writing. However, if you sometimes rush into things but at other times procrastinate, you could be a mixture of types. Where this happens, the trained graphologist has a way of working out the exact speed and how it applies to each individual.

Quick Speed

> Have you ever met someone who has left
> with an unusual feeling, a sense
> and not just because of their physi
> but because of that 'thing' — som
> intangible that makes that perso
> to you?   I have.   I can it still

Quick

POSITIVE OR GENERAL MEANINGS

Adaptable
Energetic and enthusiastic
Natural personality-vivacious
Quick grasp of the essential
Quick thinker with active mind
Spontaneous

NEGATIVE

Impatient
Impulsive
Liable to make hasty mistakes
Prone to neglect details
Quick to learn but can soon forget
Restless and prone to irritability

fast and illegible

neat and slow...

Slow Speed

> The quick brown fox jumps over the lazy dog."
>
> As you know, It contains every letter of the alphabet – so very apt for my work.

Slow

POSITIVE OR GENERAL MEANINGS

Calm and steady disposition
Conscientious
Precise
Proceeds with care and caution
Slow to learn but retains knowledge

NEGATIVE

Hides true feelings
Inhibited
Slow speed of thought and actions

Medium Speed

> I know that I have to resolve a particular problem piece of work which has been preying on my mind, but I do not have the information that I require in order to sort the job out. Consequently I deal with minor things, some of which could easily wait, while I know that I must deal with the

Medium

POSITIVE OR GENERAL MEANINGS

Moderate pace
Some people fluctuate between quick and slow

Chapter 2(h)   Rhythm

upbeat and lively

We all have our own rhythm which links internal factors (feelings, impulses and mentality) to the way we function and deal with life. This rhythm is reflected in our handwriting. This is quite an advanced stage of handwriting analysis, so don't worry if you can't spot it straight away. It may help if you try and look at the writing as a whole, rather than breaking the letters down. Ignore individual movements such as size, slant, letter shapes, etc. and simply concentrate on gaining an overall impression of the style and page as a whole. Turn the page upside down or view it from the reverse so that you get a new perspective on the whole arrangement.

stilted and rigid

GOOD RHYTHM

Rhythmic

A rhythmic style is shown in movements which appear natural, even and flowing in one direction.   The overall arrangement will be consistent with a regular recurrence of movement over the page. There should be no sudden awkward jerks or change of slant.   A rhythmic style is a sign that the writer has sufficient self-discipline and willpower to overcome unwanted feelings.   Inner balance and harmony are achieved which enables that person to ease their way through life. When problems do occur, this type has the ability to deal with them and move on with their lives. Unfortunately, rhythmic writing is quite rare these days owing to pressurised lives and jobs. If only more of us could harness inner balance and harmony; dealing with stressful lifestyles would seem easier to deal with.

Rhythmic

There are few things in this life as beautiful
as flowers. And springtime is such a
spectacular canvas for them! Magnolia
trees, cherry blossom, waving daffodils,
fragrant hyacinths, trees bursting with
fresh green buds. Wonderful.

Slightly Arrhythmic or Lively Rhythm

The style here is still rhythmic but with lively undercurrents which give it
a slight unevenness and jerkiness as the writing moves forwards.
Arrhythmic writers tend to be energetic and possess keen minds which
are capable of creative ideas. They are individualists who shun too
much convention and can appear slightly on edge.

I was fortunate as I also got to know her. But
to know her was to love her. To love a
special soul, a beautiful soul.

True beauty can be found in such souls.
It fulfills the wants and desires that
we yearn for and enables us not just to
see things but to really look at them
and identify constituent parts like never

POOR RHYTHM

Rather Arrhythmic or Chaotic

The unevenness and jerkiness in this style of writing is more pronounced as it lacks flow and harmony. Expect to see erratic slant and baselines. These types are often rather restless or excitable and they may feel off-centre. What they strive to attain is harmony and balance in their lives which can seem elusive. Set-backs can seem hard to deal with, so life continues to be an endless struggle.

Stilted or Rigid

Writing which is rather stiff, rigid and static in appearance indicates that these people have some underlying need for control in their lives. They find it difficult to totally relax because they fear that something will go wrong if they do and they can be rather compulsive. Their lives are very ordered and structured which is their way of remaining in control. A sudden change of plan is likely to cause panic.

Chapter 2(i)   Miscellaneous Movements

There are many miscellaneous movements so I have chosen just a few examples to illustrate here. The main point to make about such movements is that they may or may not have any specific psychological meaning. **One individual movement on its own means nothing and should be repeated throughout the script to have any significance.** Even then, miscellaneous movements are used to back up and confirm major movements such as size, slant, pressure and letter shapes.

DIACRITICS ('i' dots and 't' bars) The saying which says: "Watch how you dot your 'i's and cross your 't's" is quite correct. The correct placing and formation does indicate how careful we are with detail. Diacritics also reveal a wealth of information in terms of goal setting, willpower, attitude towards time, orderliness and much more.

Position of 't' bar crossing on stem - low, medium and high: Relates to height of goals set, e.g. high 't' bars = high goals.

't' bar crossing placed high above stem: Reflects high ideals which may sometimes be unrealistic.

Long 't' bar crossing: Determination, energy, enthusiasm, willpower.

Average 't' bar crossing: Healthy balance and self-control, practical approach in carrying through plans.

Short 't' bar crossing: Allows others to take the lead, lack of willpower, poor self-esteem, timidity.

't' bars & 'i' dots - placed to the right: A quick mind which looks to the future or impatience.

t' bars & 'i' dots - placed to the left: Caution or procrastination, concerned with the past.

'i' dots placed immediately over the stem indicate: Attention to detail, good memory and concentration, order, methodical, precise.

'i' dots placed high above the stem: Great imagination and enthusiasm.

'i' dots omitted altogether: Ability to delegate or absent-mindedness.

Circle 'i' dots: Artistic (not fine art forms), creative, often seen in the writing of adolescent girls, desire for attention, in a man's script - feminine trait.

OVALS

Ovals are an indication of our social inclinations, how we communicate and emotional expression.

 Always open at top: Communicative, friendly, lacks reserve so poor keeper of secrets, loves fresh air, sociable.

Occasionally open at top: Friendly and sociable but with ability to keep a secret.

 Always closed at top: Inhibited and uncommunicative.

 Locked with double loops: Complex and prone to secrecy.

 Open to left: Liable to talk about others behind their back.

 Open to right: Likely to speak one's mind and can be tactless.

 Open along baseline: Cunning and deceitful, selfish motives, sign of embezzler.

UPPER ZONE AND LOWER ZONE FORMATIONS
Upper zone

 Normal rounded loops: Emotional balance, imagination.

 Large, exaggerated loops: Day-dreamer, fantasy, overly emotional.

 Narrow loops: Intellectual with keen mind, realistic, lack of imagination.

 Retraced loops (covering stroke): Emotional and intellectual inhibition.

Lower zone

Normal loops followed through: Fulfilled, receptive and warm.

Loop not followed through: Unable to face up to problems.

Full rounded loop: Materialistic.

Short loop: Diminished sexual interest.

Claw or arc: Avoidance of physical, material or sexual responsibility.

Open to left: Open and affectionate but can be immature.

SIGNATURES

The signature is something which we consciously choose and often people will practise writing it in a certain way until it is formed to their satisfaction and presents the right image. Therefore, the signature represents the public image or persona which the person wishes to present to the outside world. On the other hand, the main body of text reveals how the person actually is because the letter formations are unconscious. For this reason, it is difficult to analyse a signature on its own because it doesn't give a complete picture of the person's character. However, I positively love receiving junk mail which has been signed by celebrities because the signatures reveal much about the way they like to be seen. Given below are a few examples of how text and signatures interact with each other.

Signature larger than the text and underlined

These writers like to appear confident and seek recognition for their efforts.

of the great things about the journey, or so I thought.

James Brill

Signature smaller than the text

The writer prefers to keep a low profile and tends to be rather modest and enjoys privacy.

certainly ending up with a recognisable situation.

John Brown

Signature similar to rest of script (both legible)

Natural personality; the writer is very much as he/she appears without putting on an act.

and I hope to see you all in the very near future.

William Bishop

Illegible writing and signature

Often due to impatience but illegibility is a form of inconsiderateness if the writer does not care if the message is legible and clear. When this occurs, it can be a form of arrogance or an unstable personality.

Legible writing with illegible signature

Despite the clear message in the main body of writing, an illegible signature can indicate haste or a secretive nature where the writer is hiding his/her true identity.

A full-stop at the end of a signature

Watch out for people who put a full-stop at the end as they often like to have the last word!

THE CAPITAL 'I' - PERSONAL PRONOUN 'I' (PPI)

Whilst the signature is a conscious choice, the PPI is formed unconsciously. This personal symbol reveals much about the writer's self-image and is susceptible to change. If something has happened to deplete confidence levels, the PPI is likely to diminish in size. Once self-esteem is restored, the PPI should increase in size again. Below are a few PPI examples and some basic interpretations. The size of the PPI is compared against the signature and size of capital letters.

Printed: Independent, confident, cultured.

Stick Figure: Mature, natural response, cultured.

Tall: Compensation for possible feelings of inferiority.

Small: Lack of self-confidence.

Lower case: Immature, poor self-esteem.

Big gap between PPI and next word:
Need for privacy.

Very near to next word: Need for company.

CAPITAL LETTERS GENERALLY

Capital letters in normal script (not predominantly capitals) represent the public side of writers and how he/she likes to appear; very much like the signature.

Large and elaborate: Air of authority and likes to be noticed.

Small: Hates being in the limelight, rather timid and shy.

Wide: Outgoing, self-confidence, vanity

Tall & Narrow: Ambitious but restricted and inhibited, narrow-minded

COLOUR OF INK

Most people commonly write in dark blue or black but there are many different colours available. Only where writers habitually choose to write in one of these unusual colours does it speak volumes about them. The general interpretations are as follows:

Black is considered more businesslike than any other colours because it represents formality and/or a demanding personality.

Royal blue is regarded as having a personal touch.

Light blue indicates a more sensitive and gentle nature.

Green can indicate a desire to be different or superior in some way. Often the writer will have strong mental and intellectual ability which can be linked to an investigative mind. Interestingly, investigators employed by banks use green ink which only they are allowed to use.

Red is often used by all sorts of professions as a way of making corrections which is not unusual. However, when someone predominantly writes in red ink the interpretation becomes more significant and has been compared to the act of shouting. It often indicates people who wish to draw attention to themselves through their behaviour, e.g. making rude remarks designed to shock or cause embarrassment.

Turquoise is a feminine colour but it can be used by those associated with artistic abilities.

Violet is associated with fashion and young women who are emotionally immature and want to improve their social standing.

A mixture of colours on one page can indicate a desire to be different or mental disorders.

Summary of Lesson

Now that you have an idea of what some of the movements mean, the important thing to bear in mind is that this is only the beginning. Once you progress with your learning, you begin to appreciate that one movement on its own means very little. There needs to be at least three movements with the same interpretation to have any real meaning, e.g. large size, right slant, broad letters and rising baselines indicate ambition.

Also, there is a great deal of psychology involved and the middle section of the course included the theories of Jung, Freud, Adler, Maslow and Fromm linked in with handwriting movements. These theories are not specifically covered in this book as readers would probably fall asleep! However, they are essential elements in understanding personalities and behaviour so that an in-depth analysis can be produced.

Once you have mastered the basics of graphology and understand how the movements link together, your mind jumps one step ahead when you meet someone new. Straight away your mind is racing ahead as you begin to wonder what their handwriting is like as their personality unfolds.

More information on handwriting movements, their interpretation and personality types are covered in Chapters 4 and 5.

Chapter 3   Frequently Asked Questions

Q1. Can graphology foretell the future?
No, it can only determine what potential a person
has and therefore what they might do
with their lives.

**Q2. Why does my handwriting
change so much?** It is quite normal for a
person's writing to fluctuate.   Young people's
handwriting often varies until they settle down, mature and develop
their own style.   Even then, style can differ because each time we write
we are influenced by our inner feelings, emotions and moods of that
moment.   A person's handwriting will vary depending on whether they
are just writing a quick note for the milkman or making an effort filling
out an application form.

**Q3. Is it possible to produce an accurate analysis from
variable handwriting?** Yes, it is. Regardless of how neat or untidy
the writing appears, the basic structure still remains.   Movements such
as the size, pressure, letter shapes, spacing and zonal ratios will be
similar.   The samples shown next were written by the same writer with a
10 year gap.   She changed to the disconnected style because she felt it
increased legibility.   Whilst the two styles look quite different, there are
more similarities than you would think, e.g. size, slant, zonal ratios and
word spacing.   The main difference is the disconnection which means
that she is now much more open and receptive to what is happening
around her.   The connected style indicates that she probably got rather
caught up in her own thoughts.

> The apparatus used in this experiment, with the subject
> relaxed standing position, was a flexi-curve. The flex
> was placed from the buttock crease upwards, along t.
> of the spine. It was then transferred to paper and t
> curve traced. When all 14 subjects had been measured

> terraced street. It dates back to
> the Victorian era & is currently in
> need of modernization. The kitchen
> is particularly bad and will need to be
> replaced entirely. It would appear that
> some of the wiring has been replaced

The example given next is in fact one sample and was written by a man in his 30's. At the time of writing he was going through an upheaval in his life with regard to his career.   This piece was written on one occasion and shows differing styles as it progresses down the page. It reveals much about his mood and attitude changes at the time of writing and his life in general. Graphologists are taught not to take into account the content but in this case it provides additional information. He begins with a right slant, rising baselines and angles which indicates a positive and competitive frame of mind. Half way down the page his competitive edge disappears as he talks about going home. The different styles helped to provide me with more clues as to his physical and mental wellbeing.   There was also valuable information about his strengths, weaknesses and potential. As can be seen from this sample, it is possible to produce an analysis from differing styles of writing.

It was a lovely lazy Sunday, woke up late,
a large breakfast.
I had booked a badminton court at bangor ee
play with a friend, got there at 12.25, just fu
before we were due to play.
I won all the games, n/b played for a long time
remember the last time was at School.

Normally we would go down the pub after wa
a few pints, but since it was mothers day w
decided to go home.

I went onto the Internet to check out my e
also checked out the BBC web site t
up on world news, and bit of sport
Also checked out the corel auction web
to see if there was any upright vacuum cl
for sale, as I need to replace mine.

Q4.   I hardly write these days and prefer using the computer, so does handwriting still play a part in our modern society?   Yes, writing is still important for the following reasons:-

1)   Whilst email and text messages have revolutionised the way we communicate with each other, handwriting still does play a part.   There are still occasions when only pen and paper will do such as letters of condolence, formal RSVP replies, thank you letters and a special note to a friend.   In any case, a personal message in a card is always welcome.

2)   There are also many employers who look at the handwriting of candidates to assess neatness and legibility.   Even without a graphological assessment, they feel the writing reveals so much about candidates (also see Chapter 4 - Recruitment).

3)   A useful tip; if you want to remember something, then write it down.   To doubly make sure, concentrate on forming small letters and this will focus the mind.

Q5.   My writing looks similar to another family member, so will it have the same interpretation?   It is not uncommon for family members to have similar traits and therefore some aspect of the writing may be similar.   It is rare for handwriting to be exactly the same, although it might look like it is on first inspection.   A person's handwriting can be compared to fingerprints in that it is totally unique to them.

Q6. Should twin's handwriting be similar? Like everyone else, each twin has their own personality and so their handwriting will differ too. However, there can be some similarities, as explained in Q5. In the samples below supplied by twin sisters in their 50's, the writing looks quite different, although the lower zone is large in both cases indicating an emphasis in that area of their lives (refer to Chapter 2a - Zones). The top sample was written by the slightly older sister and her writing is more angular indicating dominance. The younger twin was the more reserved and quiet of the two which can be seen in the prominent left slant.

Q7. Why do some people write solely in block capitals?
People often write in block capitals because they work in a profession where neat legible handwriting is paramount, such as design, engineering or accountancy.   However, some people have been known to take offence at the use of block capitals because they feel it is the equivalent of BEING SHOUTED AT!   However, John Beck, Graphologist undertook research into the subject and his studies revealed that many block capital writers are men and particularly those associated with uniforms or sports. For instance, the police, regular or Territorial Army reserves, rugby players, weight-lifters and body builders. Further reading is contained within: 'John Beck: Collected Papers on Handwriting Movements and Jungian Graphology' published by the British Institute of Graphologists.

Q8. Does the content of the sample have any bearing on the analysis?   Normally, no, we are taught to disregard the content because it can be misleading. The handwriting movements are the most important aspect, although occasionally content can add extra information as mentioned in Q3.

Q9. What is required to do an analysis?

●	Preferably a few paragraphs of writing, plus a signature (see Chapter 2(i) - Signatures) which must be representative of the writer's normal script. This should be a spontaneous piece, written as freely as you would speak. People often want to copy something but that slows down the pen movements and can interfere with the natural flow of the pen and subsequently free expression.

- The writing should be done on plain paper so that baseline direction and spacing can be assessed.

- Originals should be submitted because photocopies lose vital information such as pressure.

Additional information required:-

- The writer's approximate age and nationality (particularly the country where they were educated). This information enables the graphologist to ascertain what school copymodel they were taught to write. When individuals mature and develop their own style, this is when their personality shines through.

- The handedness of the person. This is because a left handed person tends to move the page around slightly which affects baselines and margins. It does not necessarily mean that the writer will have a left slant; I have known left-handers who have an upright or right slant.

- The gender of the writer. This is an essential piece of information if you are working on a sample from an unknown source, e.g. a newspaper to test your expertise, exams etc. Men's handwriting is often rather pointed with angular shapes and heavy pressure; women's writing tends to be rounder and softer indicating femininity. However, we are all made up of masculine and feminine tendencies, so if a woman is a high flyer, then she is likely to have more angularity in her writing. Where a man is not particularly aggressive, the movements will often look softer or curved, e.g. arcade, garland or thread formations. (Refer to Chapter 2(e) Letter Shapes and Style).

Q10. Is it possible to analyse handwriting from around the world? Yes, it is, provided it is written in a language and alphabet which is familiar to the graphologist. Whilst graphologists are taught not to pay too much attention to the content, it is essential to know what the letters mean and to spot any differences in style not specified by copymodel. For instance, the letter 'r' is often formed in a 'v' or 'n' formed as a 'u'. Countries such as Japan, China, India and Israel have their own graphologists who are familiar with their writing systems. More information on this subject can be found in: 'Graphology Across Cultures: A Universal Approach to Graphic Diversity' Edited by Dafna Yalon, published by the British Institute of Graphologists.

Q11. Is it possible to change your personality by changing your writing? Yes, there is a field of graphology called graphotherapy. It is possible for the sub-conscious mind to respond to changes in handwriting by understanding how personality traits are reflected in our writing. Negative personality traits can be improved by modifying specific strokes to bring about positive attributes such as increasing willpower, concentration, self-confidence etc. For instance, a short and weak looking 't' bar can indicate weak willpower whereas strong 't' bars with a healthy length indicate willpower and determination. Therefore, in order to favour this characteristic, the writer could practice incorporating strong 't' bars into their script. Initially the movement should be exaggerated until the influence is ingrained into the personality. Once this has happened the stronger trait will automatically be incorporated into the person's behaviour and there will be no need to consciously exaggerate the movement unless there has been a relapse. This is only a brief explanation and the procedure should be supervised by a professional graphologist.

At the very least, there needs to be a thorough understanding of how personality traits are reflected in our writing before embarking on any self-improvement exercises. This is an ideal method to help iron out problems in children and adults. To find out more about this subject read: 'Grapho-Therapeutics: Pen and Pencil Therapy' by Paul de Sainte Colombe.

Q12. Why do Doctors write illegibly? For an explanation on the legibility or illegibility of writing see Chapter 2(g). Doctors are often in a hurry and perhaps assume that the pharmacist will know what the prescription says, although these days most prescriptions are computer generated. It is often the case that highly intelligent individuals with a lively mind write illegibly purely because their writing can't keep up with their thoughts. However, in some cases it could be a case of arrogance or even an inconsiderate nature that the writer is making no effort to ensure the reader can read the message.

Q13. Is it possible to identify dishonesty from handwriting? Yes, it is, but only a trained graphologist has the expertise to decide whether a script has dishonesty signs or not. Some graphology books give a list of movements but it is quite common to see one or two in most people's handwriting and they mean nothing. As with all traits gleaned through handwriting analysis, we look for backup movements and interpretations to confirm our findings. In fact, during training, we are taught to look for at least four dishonesty signs before suspicions are aroused. Further signs would not automatically point towards an offence being committed; it just means that the person is more open or susceptible.

Even then, it is wise to tread carefully because some of the movements could be caused through ill health. For recruitment purposes, a verbal report would be given with a strong suggestion that references should be sought from previous employers.

Q14. Have you had your own handwriting analysed? Part of the course is being able to recognise your own traits through personal analysis.   Greater understanding of yourself and the handwriting movements helps you apply them to others. However, just out of self-interest, I did ask my tutor to analyse my writing before I commenced the course. The results were quite remarkable because she pointed out many qualities including a natural interest in people and psychology, although she didn't say I should be a graphologist. Over the years the information contained in this report has proved invaluable; it helped me to recognise my strengths and weaknesses and make life changes.

Q15. Does the size of the person have any bearing on the actual size of the handwriting? No, it has no connection at all and I once worked for an engineer who had quite small and 'girly' writing and he was a giant of a man.

Q16. Can you tell if the writer is left handed? This is something we need to ascertain before starting the analysis (see Q9). Whilst there are certain movements which do indicate left handedness, they are not always present. For instance, 't' bars are often crossed from right to left, with the pointed end to the left. To make it easier to write a left hander will sometimes turn the page which affects margins and baseline direction so that it descends. It is imperative that we are not making wrong assumptions here.

Q17. How detailed is an analysis? Whilst I would not claim that it reveals everything about the personality, the information is detailed and specific to that person.   Content is adjusted to suit, e.g. a couple seeking relationship guidance are probably not so interested in their working qualities as someone seeking vocational guidance.   A section on Strengths/Weaknesses and Potential is included for vocational guidance, personal development and recruitment purposes.   An abbreviated list of typical traits covered in an analysis is listed below.

General Health & Vitality: Energy, sense of wellbeing or discontentment, stress, anxiety, willpower.

Personality Structure: Mixture of extroversion/introversion, attitudes towards time (future, present or past orientated), parental influences from childhood, independence or dependency, drive, determination, spontaneity, sensitiveness.

Social Attitudes & Reactive Behaviour: Self-confidence, shy, reserve, broad or narrow minded, approach - quick, medium or slow, impulsive or cautious, communication skills, adaptability, generous or mean, reliability, demonstrative, manner (even tempered, or restless, irritable, temperamental), sociable, friendly.

Intellectual Qualities: Logical, intuitive, analytical, ability to concentrate, creativity, imagination, memory, quick or slow thinker, perceptive, observant.

Working Qualities: Ideal role (Leader, Persuader-sales type, Perfectionist, Team Player, Original Thinker), degree of ambition, aggressiveness, attention to detail, decisiveness, goals, approach (quick/slow), method (efficient/inefficient), integrity, reliability, degree of responsibility, planning and organisation, motivation.

Chapter 4 **Company Use**

Recruitment

Organisations use graphology or handwriting analysis as a recruitment tool, although it is more widely accepted and used in countries such as France. It can be used on its own or in conjunction with psychometric testing. An analysis of this nature provides an accurate insight into the true personality and capabilities of short-listed candidates. All the candidate(s) need to do is provide a handwriting sample for analysis and the graphologist does the rest; there are no questions to answer or boxes to tick. Companies should make candidates aware that their writing is being used for this purpose. Handwritten letters of application or writing on application forms are not ideal samples to work from. This is because the writing is usually in the applicant's best writing, so what graphologists look for is a natural script which is representative of the writer's normal style. Therefore, candidates should be asked to produce a sample specifically for analysis. Also see Chapter 3, Q4 (2).

Some form of additional checking is essential, especially at senior level. Often what is seen at interviews is a façade which the candidate projects and some are very accomplished at painting an acceptable image of themselves. This could account for the fact that I meet many employers who complain that their dream employee has turned out to be a complete nightmare. What has happened is that a few weeks into the employment of this individual their true personality and capabilities are revealed and it is not what the employer was expecting.

An in-depth report can determine the suitability of candidates in terms of their overall personality, their intellect, working qualities and how they are likely to 'blend' in with the company's culture.   The graphologist first liaises with the company to obtain details of the job description and what type of person they are looking for.   The report compares these qualities against those of the candidate's.   It quickly establishes strengths and weaknesses which may not immediately be apparent and enables the company to quickly ascertain the candidate's suitability for the job.   More importantly it determines reliability and ethics, particularly important factors where handling money is concerned.   However, the graphologist's role is not to recommend who should get the job but merely to assist the company in making that final decision.

Workplace Personality Types and Team Building

For those company directors who seek to surround themselves with people just like themselves, this is likely to result in disaster.   An important element of any company striving for success is to have a broad range of types which results in better productivity and efficiency. Above all, job satisfaction and performance is increased as each individual is placed in a role which suits their personality and skills. Therefore, information on personality types would feature in any report for team building, recruitment or where an individual is looking for vocational guidance.

There are many ways of typecasting people and putting them into categories, e.g. Myers Briggs Type Indicator® based on Jung's theory of psychological types, Belbin Team Profiling, D-I-S-C, the Enneagram etc.

The course I completed with the British Institute of Graphologists covered five types commonly found within the workplace: Leader, Persuader, Team Player, Perfectionist and Original Thinker (illustrated below).   These types provide a basic framework to build in other traits from other systems.   However, not all the traits apply within a given category, so it is down to the skill of the graphologist to judge which ones apply.   Therefore, it is possible for individuals to 'lend' themselves to more than one role if traits overlap.   The more keen-eyed reader is likely to spot that I have duplicated handwriting samples to illustrate different personality types or professions (see Chapter 5).

Leader types

Whilst there are different types of leaders, they have certain traits in common.   They generally like to take control and get results because that is why they are there.   How they get the results depends on their approach and how they relate to and see others.   Some handwriting movements to look out for in a typical leader: medium to large size, upright or right slant, medium to heavy pressure, some angles at least and connected letters.

Different Leader types:-

Bully: During our working careers, many of us will experience a boss with a bullying temperament. They're domineering hard-line types and they don't really care very much if they upset people along the way. It is not surprising that they leave a lasting impression. They won't listen to what their workforce has to say and will consider suggestions to be tantamount to treason. Below is a sample of a bullying boss who likes to get his own way and does not welcome the opinion of others. Note the harsh angular lines, large size, heavy pressure which indicate resistance and dominance.

Firm approach: Below is the handwriting of an individual who has great presence, energy and authority which is shown in the large size, large lower zone, upright/right slant and heavy pressure. Firmness is indicated in the angle and arcade forms of connection, although the angularity is not as severe as the previous sample.

Democratic: The next sample is of a more democratic and fair-minded individual who adopts a softly-softly approach which can be seen in the garland forms of connection and occasional threading. The emphasis here is on being open to what others have to say, although this is not to say this type is a push-over because ultimately they will have the last word. This writer shows physical and mental strength which can be seen in the medium/heavy pressure, stable baselines and some angles.

Have you ever met someone who has
with an unusual feeling, a fun
and not just because of their play
but because of that 'thing' - so
intangible that makes that pers

Whichever type of leader you work for, make sure you are well prepared and act confidently when you meet them. They are purpose driven, so be to the point and don't try and pull the wool over their eyes.

Persuader (sales & training)

This type is well placed in a sales or training environment because they are excellent relationship builders and motivators. Their strengths lie in quickly getting to know people and forging business relationships. They promote products or services with ease and operate smoothly by persuading others to purchase. So, before you know where you are you've bought whatever they are selling. They enjoy being with people, so if you work with someone who is constantly on the phone when they're in the office or away from their desk, then they have some Persuader characteristics. Their preference is to be out and about and they hate mundane paperwork because their concentration levels are low. Give them a form to fill in or a pile of filing and you could wait forever. Regulations are not for them because they will bend a rule in order to meet your requirements and bring about a favourable result.

Handwriting movements to look out for: large size, right slant, firm pressure and rising baseline. The three samples I have chosen are all from individuals who have the quality of easily building working relationships and helping others, although none of them are pure Persuader types.

The example shown below is a combination of Leader and Persuader types.   This is because the writing has many of the movements mentioned above, plus angular letter shapes.   Angles provide this female manager with a very firm and dynamic personality.   This lady has plenty of motivation and presence.   Whilst persuasion is not necessarily her style, she is very enthusiastic and passionate about life and quickly builds workplace relationships.   These are her Persuader traits and it is these qualities which she uses to encourage others to achieve higher goals and succeed.

The next example is obviously that of an extrovert character with a preference for group involvement at most levels.   The combination of angles and garlands provide him with firmness and charm - another Leader/Persuader type.   He uses his boundless energy and enthusiasm to lead and inspire others to succeed.   It is not surprising that his strengths lie in building customer relations, selling, leading and training.

> Red is Directive task focused and dri
> Blue is helpful and friendly, good with p
> Green is Detailed and Analytical
> Yellow is a mixture of all 3 in almost
> and are great in team situations and
> fill in for missing colours

The threads in this next sample indicate smoothness in interpersonal relationships and the ability to see an easy, trouble-free path. Interestingly, this writer has also ended up working with people and helping individuals find their true vocation.

> I studying 'fine art' at Brighton
> sity and Dieu, whe D at
> Hford University studying psychology.
> have a small yacht. She D a
> 34 which I keep at Emsworth w
> ter Harbour. She D huge fun
> very relaxing when used in Summe

PERFECTIONIST

Perfectionist

Perfectionists like everything to be done properly and to be in its place and this is how their handwriting appears; neat and tidy. They have an incredible eye for detail, so they are very well placed in a working environment where care and attention to detail are essential. Being very capable and competent are all positive personality traits in the right working environment. Working in a situation which requires too much haste and instant adjustment is not for them. This is because their main priority is excellence of work and nothing else will do. Having to rush something and cut corners in order to complete a task would offend them greatly. Their safety zone is staying with the familiar and observing rules and regulations.

This is an example of a Perfectionist's writing. Legible, clear, neat and tidy — orderly too — just like the writer.

Please find a couple of paragraphs written totally off the top of my head — hope it makes the book!

It reminds me that, just as springtime follows winter, light will follow dark and good times will follow bad. And so the

I felt it was a shame there was no one special in her life. She had a couple of failed romances behind her which I think

Original Thinker

These types are excellent at coming up with new ideas, so they are valued by any company who needs creative ideas for their new lines. They can become quite 'lost' in their own thoughts because they are caught up in their own world of imagination. When working on a project, they like to keep to themselves and hand over the finished product when they are satisfied with it. Given a remit they will work continuously until it is finished but they need to be gently reminded of any looming deadline because they won't notice. They hate too many restrictions, so rules and regulations are not for them.

Original thinking can be shown up in different ways. Either the writing will be of the larger variety or irregular in some way but do not expect to find small, neat and tidy writing as would be expected with the Perfectionist type.

when I escaped from mother and
ran off down Brickhill Drive i Bedford
only to be found by police and
brought home i squad car . . . .

Please find enclosed handwriting Samples plus che
for £60-00 as agreed.
My husband will not be able to make it, the
                        is taking his place for the evening
Parents will also be there.)
We are very much looking forward to t
evening.

Team Player

Companies value team
players because they are persistent in
tackling tasks and are loyal employees.
They get on with their day by working in a methodical and deliberate
way, although, like the perfectionist, they hate being rushed. Refining
existing practices is a speciality because they hate unnecessary
change. They're good listeners and can get on with all sorts of people
because they are not confrontational.   Ever thoughtful and
considerate types, they hate firing someone or delegating because
they fear overloading other people. If negative traits appear, then
they can be rather suspicious and they will hide their anger which
means they can suddenly explode!

Typical handwriting movements to look out for: Medium size,
garlands, legible, medium/slow speed, fairly regular, good spacing,
straight baselines. **Some of these movements are present in
the sample below.**

A few weeks ago I went to the wedding
of a girl I have worked with. A girl I
have liked and admired + made a friend of.
In fact, since my first days of working for
the Company I have known her + took to
her niceness & warmth.
She lit her 30th birthday last year + whilst
quite happy in her life she has a married
elder brother + lived at home with her parents—
I felt it was a shame there was no one

Chapter 5 **Professions and Handwriting Styles**

The aim of this chapter is to show how personality traits reveal themselves in the handwriting of certain professions. Only a small selection has been used to provide examples. The intention is to give the reader an idea of how graphology works in the workplace.

CHARTERED SURVEYOR

An example shown below is that of a chartered surveyor. I temped as his secretary for a couple of weeks and also worked for another surveyor, so I found this type of script fairly typical of the profession. Some of his traits were similar to that of a Perfectionist, e.g. attention to detail and observing rules and regulations. However, these qualities alone would not provide him with the ability to carry out all his duties, which amounted to a very busy schedule. He needed management skills and to work at great speed. Listed below are some of the handwriting movements and characteristics which helped him carry out his duties.

This example is written quickly which means that he operates at great speed. However, the left slant shows caution so he is less likely to make an impulsive mistake. The small compact middle zone letters indicate good powers of concentration and the low 'i' dot also confirms a good memory and attention to detail.

Wide line spacing shows clear thought processes and the ability to plan and organise. The pressure is firm indicating good energy levels, so he is able to keep up momentum and deal with a heavy workload. Baselines are straight and slightly rising, so good self-control and optimism are evident.

THE BOSS

The next sample is of another surveyor and imagine my surprise when it dropped out of the envelope! Having accustomed myself to the previous style of writing and feeling it was fairly typical of the profession, I was really surprised to see this expansive script indicating a smattering of Persuader/Leader/Original Thinker types. I obviously felt that he was in the wrong profession because the Persuader loves social contact and forging workplace relationships. Their focus is on the big picture which is confirmed in the very large style. Typically, they hate being confined in any way by attending to detail and following rules and regulations. The Leader Type likes to take control and get results, so a good combination if the writer is the boss.

I was sent the script to comment on as part of a talk to the local surveyors club, so I thought I'd better speak to the writer in case I was about to make a horrible mistake! He immediately confirmed what I suspected, that he had started life as a surveyor and hated it because he felt too restricted. He quickly realised his mistake and started his own company which suits his Persuader/Leader/Original style of thinking. Fortunately he has an excellent team and PA dealing with all the intricacies of the profession while he gets on with managing the business.

ADMINISTRATORS/PERSONAL ASSISTANTS

The previous personality type needs a good personal assistant or Perfectionist/Team Player to organise his day and make sure that nothing is overlooked. The samples shown below indicate excellent administrative ability and interpersonal skills because the writing is neatly laid out, clearly spaced and legible. In fact, the first job I had as an office junior had me working for such a paragon of virtue. She was a stickler for order and everything being done properly. Fairly recently I found a sample of her handwriting and it amused me because it was so typical of a Perfectionist's writing.

> Please find a couple of paragraphs
> written totally off the top of my head
> - hope it makes the book !

> It reminds me that, just as springtime
> follows winter, light will follow dark and
> good times will follow bad. And so the

> I felt it was a shame there was no one
> special in her life. She had a couple of
> failed romances behind her which I think

DESIGNERS

Both of these samples have been written by designers and they show a large degree of perfectionism, although the style is fairly typical of people I meet who have artistic or designing ability.   The letters are precisely formed with an emphasis on angular or arcade shapes and the whole layout is pleasing and well thought through.   The writer of the 'Dear Joyce…' sample has adopted her own particular distinctive and artistic way of writing the letter 'D' (also the first letter of her signature - not shown) and 'a' which shows style and attention to detail.

Dear Joyce,
*   I have been wondering what I could write for you, and at last something springs to mind!*
" The quick brown fox jumps over the lazy dog."
As you know, It contains every letter of the alphabet - so very apt for my work.

> This is a sample of my normal (not calligraphic) handwriting. If I try really hard I can produce quite acceptable calligraphy, but this is easier and faster.
>
> If I'm just making notes for myself, my writing is much more of a scrawl, and sometimes almost illegible, except to myself.
>
> Regards my signature, I devised it specifically when I was 16, and it's stuck!

COMMUNICATIONS

Marketing Writer /PR Consultant

I also placed the next sample under 'Administrators and Personal Assistants' because this writer is organised, orderly and operates to high standards. Her thoughts are separated out and she clearly communicates her ideas - see legible style, arcades, good layout, clear line spacing. However, there is more to this Perfectionist type than administration because she is a professional writer who specialises in coming up with fresh words and ideas for marketing material.

There's a great deal of warmth in the rounded letters which show her ability to reach out to other people and communicate her message. She has good self-control which is a must when working for yourself, otherwise you'd never get anything done - see straight baselines, regular, strong 't' bars. The upright style points towards independence and self-sufficiency, so she is able to manage on her own. There's also a degree of cautiousness, so she is careful about taking major decisions and is not likely to act impulsively.

There are few things in this life as beautiful as flowers. And springtime is such a spectacular canvas for them! Magnolia trees, cherry blossom, waving daffodils, fragrant hyacinths, trees bursting with fresh green buds. Wonderful.

It reminds me that, just as springtime follows winter, light will follow dark and good times will follow bad. And so the cycle repeats. It's the wheel of life. It's inevitable! Behind the clouds the sun is always there.

COMMUNICATIONS

PR Consultant

The sample below is of a businesswoman who runs her own PR company. Speed of thought and creative thinking is key in her line of work. Firstly, the rapid pace it has been written and the simplified letters confirms her speed of thought and the sharp horizontal crossings on 'i' & 't' indicate a sharp wit! There is plenty of movement in the writing indicating adaptability, so she is instantly able to change direction without too much trouble. Typical of an Original Thinker is her liking for variety, so she probably dislikes too much red tape and sticking to restrictive rules and regulations. Her individuality and freedom of thought are necessary components of her working life. The clear spacing between the lines confirms clear thinking and the ability to plan and organise. The only down side is that the pressure is fairly weak pointing towards lack of sustained energy and stamina. However, the change of letter shapes from angles, arcades and threads again indicate speed of thought and the ability to charm her way out of situations. In other words, she is making life easy for herself and does not need to use unnecessary force or energy to get her way.

Manners, began at the age of two when I escaped from mother and ran off down Brickhill Drive i Bedford only to be found by police and brought home i squad car ....

MEDICAL HERBALIST

The sample shown below is of a Medical Herbalist who runs her own business.   Imagination is shown in the large upper zone loops and the large absolute size indicates a need for freedom to expand and make the most of her creativity. Maintaining individuality is paramount and being confined by too much convention or restrictive situations is not for her.   A well developed upper zone indicates an active mind but she also has small middle zone letters which shows the ability to concentrate on her important work as a Medical Herbalist.

Please find enclosed handwriting samples plus cheque
for £60-00 as agreed.
My husband will not be able to make it, therefore
_____ is taking his place for the evening — (his
Parents will also be there.)
We are very much looking forward to the
evening.
I did not realise you wanted unlined paper & so
did not pass that info on — sorry.

MENTAL HEALTH CARER/NURSE

The example shown below is from a writer who is training to be a mental health carer. Wide letters indicate a sociable nature and the garland letter shapes point towards an extremely kind, sympathetic and caring disposition. There is also a natural ability to 'tune' into how others feel and to empathise with them. However, the danger with pure garland types is that they have trouble distancing themselves from how their patients feel. Ideally, there should be some angles or arcades to protect the writer from becoming too emotionally involved and taking their work home with them.

SOLICITORS, ENGINEERS and ACCOUNTANTS

Many of the experts in this category could fall into the Perfectionist category because all of these professions require precision, following rules and regulations, organisational ability, persistence and a high degree of competency.   However, they all have their individual movements and traits which they need to carry out their tasks.   For instance, management ability is necessary if the engineer is in a charge of others.

In my early days as a secretary, I worked for a brilliant engineer but his management and communication skills were lacking.   This was way before I knew anything about graphology but I was amused at his tiny little writing.   It looked a bit 'girly' to me, particularly as he was rather a giant of a man who used to block the light when standing in the doorway.   Small writing indicates an introverted personality and he was certainly very quiet and hardly ever came out of his office.   It was hard work trying to get any form of conversation out of him and I did feel that this affected his ability to communicate and manage his team. However, he was obviously in the right type of job because the small writing provided him with the ability to concentrate for long periods of time and pay attention to detail.   A typical Perfectionist!

Below is just a small sample of professionals I have encountered within the legal and accountancy field.   Another book is required to illustrate variations in personality, intellect and working qualities.

SOLICITOR AND LEGAL DIRECTOR

The following example is from a Legal Director and this solicitor specialises in conveyancing and Wills. Therefore, intellectual and management qualities are essential and his writing featured under Leader types - the democratic variety shown in Chapter 4.

This solicitor's personality is like his writing style - natural, energetic, spontaneous and genuine! His mannerisms are quick and lively and so is his mind.

An astute mind is indicated which is capable of brilliant ideas and acquiring knowledge. His mind seeks constant stimulation otherwise he will soon become bored. Despite dealing with routine matters, he still appreciates variety and change in his life - see quick and legible writing style.

Clear spacing and stable baselines show the ability to plan and organise effectively. He also has a healthy attitude towards planning for the future and is open to new ideas and opportunities - see natural style, broad letters and narrow right margin.

A flexible attitude is indicated in that he is able to change in response to difficult situations and avoid confrontations. This aspect also means he is immediately at ease with people in all walks of life - see quick speed, lively rhythm, some threading.

Firm pressure, stable baselines and lively rhythm indicate an abundance of energy and vitality. These qualities provide him with stamina and the ability to keep on track.

> Have you ever met someone who has left you with an unusual feeling, a sense of 'wow! and not just because of their physical beauty but because of that 'thing' – something intangible that makes that person special to you? I have. I saw it, felt it and realised it, even before I knew her!
>
> I was fortunate as I also got to know her. But to know her was to love her. To love a special soul, a beautiful soul.

ACCOUNTANT

This next example is from an accountant who has vast experience working in senior management positions. Therefore, his writing shows precision and the ability to lead - his writing features under the Leader Types in Chapter 4. I have also seen similar styles of writing from engineers who need similar qualities in terms of management and attention to detail.

The large size and right slant indicate a confident, outgoing and sociable personality which provides him with leadership qualities and the ability to forge working relationships. Heavy pressure and some angularity provide him with firmness so he is able to stand his ground.

There is the ability to plan and organise effectively and a good memory is indicated. Actions are thought through logically and systematically- see right slant, good layout, connected, regular style. However, there are occasions when his mind can become a little muddled due to his increasing workload which can be seen in the large lower zone 'y' 'g' which mingles with line below.

A keen mind is indicated, so he is able to deal with complex situations and is likely to feel frustrated and stifled without challenges of a mentally stimulating nature - see well developed upper zone and connected letters.

The right slant and legibility show a keen sense of duty and responsibility towards others, so he can be relied upon to be loyal and trustworthy. In addition, there's a wish to be helpful and supportive of friends and loved ones - original shows A4 sheet with narrow margins all round. The heavy pressure and large size indicate great energy and natural authority is used to combat injustice in the home and society. The writer is happiest when totally in control of a situation and will feel restless and frustrated with events when progress seems slow. Fortunately, self discipline, willpower and determination keep his mind focused and on track.

The day started off reasonably well with a bi clear, sunny but cold morning with everyone getting up on time so that we reached the drops for buses within time. Then Jenny I walked the Pooch in Buckingham's twirls park and we parted outside the school a

Chapter 6   Individual/General Use

Vocational Guidance/Personal Development

It is often the case that greater potential lies buried within seemingly unpromising individuals for many years. However, once these seeds of greatness are recognised, they can spring to life and start people on a new path of self-discovery and success. One way of discovering inner qualities and seeing ourselves in a new light is through handwriting analysis. The information revealed in an analysis can help individuals towards a more satisfying career which makes the most of their true potential.

Whilst some people may spend many years feeling complete failures because they did not succeed at school, there are others who entered the wrong career in the first place. As a consequence, I often encounter people who are dissatisfied with their working lives. They're looking for a change of direction and a new career which is when vocational guidance is useful. An in-depth analysis provides a useful insight into the individual's personality, intellect, working qualities, strengths/weaknesses and potential. Suggestions of possible careers can then be made which take all these factors into consideration. Sometimes people know what they want to do, so it is just a matter of confirming that their chosen career path is right for them, particularly if it entails years of study.

I have also been approached by individuals who are happy within their existing field of work but wish to push themselves up the career ladder. An analysis can identify areas that hinder progress such as lack of confidence or poor self-esteem which result in low goal-setting and achievements. Self-knowledge helps individuals recognise their strengths but more importantly understand where weaknesses need to be addressed. Self-limiting beliefs can be overcome once they are identified. The aim of the analysis is not to belittle people but purely to provide the impetus and knowledge to turn a negative into a positive situation.

Relationship Compatibility

This type of report is one of the most complicated and time-consuming to produce. The procedure begins by producing two reports and then comparing traits across to assess compatibility. It is not a case of establishing if both sides are the same in all areas but whether they complement each other through differences or similarities. Where an incompatibility arises, then at least the couple are aware it exists and usually why. This knowledge helps couples to overcome problems which may not be immediately apparent. Greater understanding of each other's needs helps to build tolerance and a successful partnership.

A compatibility report is also useful to couples in a long-term relationship who have hit a rocky patch. The analysis can shed new light on behaviour patterns and difficulties which may even stem back to childhood. What this information provides is an insight into why a person is behaving in a particular way and can help with the counselling process. Also see 'Counselling - Family Experiences'.

Counselling - Family Experiences

A handwriting analysis can help therapists treat patients by providing them with background information which may otherwise be difficult to establish.   The aim is to short-circuit the counselling process by identifying the root of a problem.   However, it doesn't replace the counselling process but merely provides advance information to speed up the diagnosis and treatment.

Children - Psychological

Children's handwriting can be analysed by making allowances for uncoordinated movements causing irregular letter shapes and layout. Also, where young children are still mastering the school copymodel, letters tend to look uniformly round.   However, there are many hidden clues in children's writing which can shed new light on a problem. These issues can be difficult to pinpoint because children hide so much about themselves.   An analysis of handwriting and even doodles can reveal much about how children feel about themselves and other people.   Also revealed is an insight into their intellect, capabilities and health issues.   This information helps parents and teachers to understand children and address problems which may be difficult to pinpoint.

Children - Learning to Write

It is possible for a graphologist to work with teachers of children from 5 to 12 to help them develop writing skills in the cursive style. Teachers should learn the method first so that they can teach children to write in a fluent cursive style. Good posture and pen grip is taught too. Often children learn to write by printing each individual letter which can be difficult for them to master. This new method introduces children to writing by first forming continuous large and small loops. It is easy to master because there is no need to think about lifting the pen off the paper. They don't have to worry about forming a certain letter; they just learn fluid and continuous loops. These loops form an 'e' or 'l' and other movements are introduced until the whole alphabet is covered. Along the way, the class is encouraged to form linked letters into words. However, there are a few combinations where letters are difficult to connect, so they are left disconnected. Astonishing results have been achieved by Canadian Graphologist, Graziella Pettaniti where her expertise has been appreciated by teachers and children in Canada.

Physical/Mental Illness

Graphology can detect a variety of physical and mental illnesses as symptoms can appear in the writing before the person is actually aware a problem exists. Have you ever noticed that the quality of your writing is affected when you're feeling ill, stressed or tired? If the answer is 'yes' then you can begin to understand that physical and mental disorders affect the whole system. This is a specialised area requiring great understanding of how symptoms can appear in writing.

Stress

Stress can be a motivational factor provided levels are moderate. However, many of us lead hectic lives and are put under excessive stress at work. Some people cope with pressure more easily than others, but those that are subjected to excessive levels can become ill. A graphologist is able to detect how a person deals with outside pressures, how stressed the person actually feels and whether they are able to cope.

Drug/Alcohol Abuse

It is possible to detect the adverse effects of drug/alcohol abuse but it requires specialist knowledge as the symptoms can be due to physical or mental illness.

Police/Forensic/Document Examination

A graphologist who has trained with the British Institute of Graphologists or other recognised body is well equipped to scrutinize and measure detailed movements. This knowledge is essential in the detection of suspected forgeries and malicious letters. However, additional knowledge is necessary in the area of paper and inks etc, so this type of work is often referred to a Document Examiner. It is a specialised forensic field and some graphologists do additional training to equip them to work in this area and to become Expert Witnesses.

Miscellaneous

In addition to analysing writing and working with individuals and companies, graphologists can use their expertise in other areas:-

- Public speaking for a variety of social and business groups.

- Parties - a unique and fun way to sample handwriting analysis with a group of friends.

- Radio and TV interviews.

- Promotions - on-the-spot analysing at exhibitions and corporate events.

- Teaching/Workshops - to introduce newcomers to the subject or educate those embarking on a professional qualification.

BIBLIOGRAPHY

Handwriting Analysis

Amend, Karen & Ruiz, Mary S: *Handwriting Analysis: The Complete Basic Book* (Newcastle Publishing Co. Inc., North Hollywood, California, USA, 1980).

Amend, Karen Kristin & Ruiz, Mary Stansbury: *Achieving Compatibility with Handwriting Analysis (Vol 1)* (Newcastle Publishing Co. Inc., North Hollywood, California, USA, 1992).

Beck, John: *Collected Papers on Handwriting Movements and Jungian Graphology* (The British Institute of Graphologists, 2000).

Branston, Barry: *Graphology Explained - A Workbook* (Judy Piatkus Publishers Ltd, London, 1989).

Cohen, Frits and Wander, Daniel: *Handwriting Analysis at Work* (Thorsons, 1993).

De Sainte Colombe, Paul: *Grapho-Therapeutics: Pen and Pencil Therapy* (DeVorss & Co. California, USA, 1988).

Hargreaves, Gloria and Wilson, Peggy: *A Dictionary of Graphology: The A-Z of Your Personality* (Peter Owen Publishers, London, 1983, 1991).

Mendel, Alfred O: *Personality in Handwriting* (Newcastle Publishing Co Ltd, North Hollywood, California, USA, 1990).

Paterson, Jane: *SIGN HERE - How Significant is Your Signature?* (Ashgrove Press Ltd, Bath, 1998)

Pettinati, Graziella: *The Pleasure of Writing Well*, paper presented at the Proceedings of the Eighth British Symposium on Graphology (The British Institute of Graphologists, 2005).

Roman, Kara G: *Handwriting: A Key to Personality* (S F M Press, Columbus, Ohio, USA, 1996).

Saudek, Robert: *Experiments with Handwriting* (Books for Professionals, Sacramento, California, USA, 1978).

Yalon, Dafna (editor): *Graphology Across Cultures: A Universal Approach To Graphic Diversity* (The British Institute Of Graphologists, 2003).

Please note: Some older graphology books are out of print but may be obtained second hand via Amazon.

Psychology and Personality Types

Belbin, Meredith R: *Management Teams Why They Succeed or Fail,* (Elsevier Butterworth-Heinemann, Linacre House, Jordan Hill, Oxford, 1981, 2004).

Quenk, Naomi L: *Essentials of Myers-Briggs Type Indicator®️ Assessment,* (John Wiley & Sons, Inc, 605 Third Avenue, New York, USA, 2000).

Rohm, Robert A, Ph.D: *Positive Personality Profiles "D-I-S-C-OVER" Personality Insights to understand yourself....and others!* (Personality Insights, Inc. Atlanta, Georgia, USA, 1998).

Shultz, Duane P and Shultz, Sydney Ellen: *Theories of Personality,* (Wadsworth/Thomson Learning, Belmont, California, USA, 2001).

Webb, Karen: *The Enneagram* (Thorsons, 1996).

General

The British Institute of Graphologists' leaflet *The Guide to Graphology*.

FURTHER INFORMATION FROM:

Just Perfect Analysing Ltd, PO Box 1129, Bedford, MK40 4XT
www.jpanalysis.co.uk

INDEX